Raccoons

Elizabeth Russell-Arnot

Contents

Raccoons

Raccoons are
small animals
about the size
of a fox.

They live on the ground
and in trees,
and are found in
North and South America.

Raccoons are **nocturnal** animals.
They sleep during the day
and are awake at night.

What raccoons look like

Raccoons have thick fur and long, bushy tails with black and gray rings around them.

They have black markings,
like masks,
around the eyes and cheeks.

Raccoons look like
masked bandits!

They have
small front paws
which look like
a tiny pair of hands.

What is a raccoon's tail like?

Raccoon homes

A raccoon's home is called a **den**.

Sometimes the den is in a hollow tree. Sometimes it is a hole among rocks. It may be the old underground home of another animal, such as a skunk.

The den is a safe place for a raccoon to sleep in during the daytime.

A raccoon's tail is long and bushy with black and gray rings.

On a warm day,
a raccoon may climb into a tree
and lie in the fork of a branch,
or in an empty bird's nest.

A raccoon likes sleeping in the sun.

When does a raccoon sleep in its den?

Raccoons in autumn

During the autumn,
raccoons eat a lot of food.
They become very fat and move slowly.

When winter comes and food is scarce,
the extra fat helps them to stay alive.

Raccoons also grow a very thick
coat of fur to keep them warm.

A raccoon sleeps in its den
during the daytime.

Raccoons in winter

Raccoons that live in very cold parts of North America sleep in their dens for long periods during winter, and only come out on warmer days.

Raccoons that live in warmer places are active all year round.

Do all raccoons stay in their dens during winter?

The raccoon family

In early spring, a mother raccoon has between two and six babies.

Raccoon babies are called **cubs**.

When the cubs are born, they are very small and blind.

At about seven weeks old, the cubs leave the den for the first time.

No. Raccoons that live in warmer places are active all year round.

When the cubs are older,
their mother takes them hunting with her.
She teaches them where to find food
and how to catch it.

A mother raccoon
and her cubs keep in touch
with each other by making
all sorts of noises.
They can hiss and growl
and purr and grunt.

Cubs are very good
at climbing trees.

What do mother raccoons
teach their cubs?

Hunting for food

Many raccoons live in woodlands,
near streams and lakes,
where food is easy to find.

When it is dark,
the raccoons wake up
and leave their dens
to go hunting.

Sometimes they hunt
for mice, earthworms,
and grasshoppers.

They wade and swim
to find fish, crayfish,
tadpoles, frogs,
and turtles.

Mother raccoons teach their cubs
where to find food and how to catch it.

Raccoons use their front paws
to catch moving fish.

They can open mussel shells
with their strong fingers,
and feel for frogs hiding in the mud.

How do raccoons catch fish, frogs,
and mussels?

The masked bandit

Raccoons sometimes raid hen houses
and take eggs or young chicks.
They use their front paws
to open the hen house doors.

Raccoons will climb trees
to find birds' eggs
or baby birds.

They will tip
bird feeders over
to get at
the seeds and nuts.

Raccoons use their front paws and strong
fingers to catch fish, frogs, and mussels.

Raccoons take fruit from orchards
and vineyards, and vegetables from gardens.

Raccoons also love to eat sweet corn.
They creep into fields at night
and eat until they are very full.

What are some of the plant foods
that raccoons eat?

City raccoons

Many raccoons live in or near towns and cities.

Because they eat so many different foods, they find plenty to eat in garbage dumps and inside garbage cans.

When there is plenty of food, raccoons will eat as much as they can fit in their stomachs.

Then they will sleep for a while, wake up, and eat some more.

They do this many times.

Raccoons eat plant foods such as seeds, nuts, fruits, vegetables, and sweet corn.

Where can raccoons find food
in towns and cities?

Where raccoons live

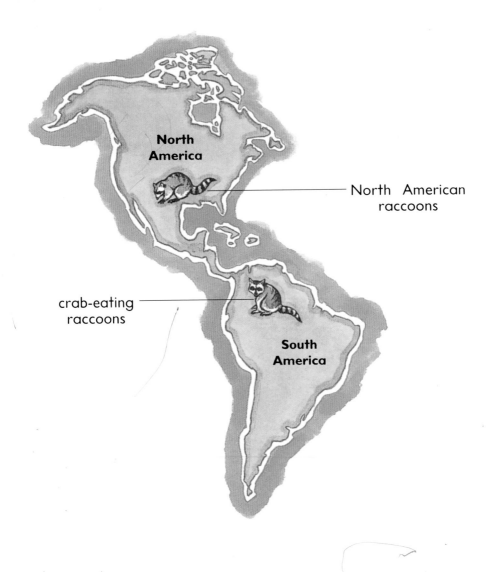

North America

North American raccoons

crab-eating raccoons

South America

Raccoons in towns and cities find food in garbage dumps and garbage cans.